Antitrust Parens Patriae Bill
Consumer damage suits by state attorneys general

American Enterprise Institute for Public Policy Research
Washington, D.C.

KF
1652
.A44

132926

ISBN 0-8447-0173-4
Legislative Analysis No. 7, 94th Congress
26 November 1975

Price $2.00 per copy

CONTENTS

BACKGROUND 1

    The Current Antitrust Drive 1
    Recent Increases in Antitrust Penalties 1
    Pending Antitrust Enforcement Bills 1
    Purpose and Scope of the Antitrust Laws 3

SUMMARY OF THE BILL 5

    The "Parens Patriae" Concept 5
    Provisions of H.R. 8532 5
    Proposals Not in the Bill 6

THE MAIN ARGUMENTS 9

    Compensation for Consumers 9
    Deterrence of Violations 13
    Mandatory Treble Damages 17
    Costs and Attorney Fees: The Question of Fairness 20
    Cases Farmed Out by the States–Contingent Fees 22

NOTES TO TEXT 25

BACKGROUND

The Current Antitrust Drive

Congressional drives to strengthen the antitrust laws have been in vogue from time to time since the turn of the century.[1] As a result, the antitrust laws "entail multiple damnations of forbidden restraints, one punishment sure if another fails."[2] As Jerrold G. Van Cise, a well-known authority on antitrust, points out, the federal antitrust statutes now include provisions for "substantial fines, years in jail, injunctions, divestiture, and treble damages...."[3] But he notes that "[t]he interest on Capitol Hill would appear rather to lie in the encouragement of more numerous enforcement proceedings and in more painful antitrust penalties."[4]

Recent Increases in Antitrust Penalties

The effort to translate the current antitrust fervor into legislation is reflected in several recent enactments and the serious consideration being given to various other antitrust proposals. For example, just a few months ago Congress increased the maximum fine for antitrust violations from $50,000 to $1 million for corporations and $100,000 for individuals and raised the maximum criminal penalty from one to three years in prison.[5] Another measure in the antitrust area, signed into law during the last (93d) Congress, increased the penalties for violating orders of the Federal Trade Commission (FTC), strengthened the powers of the FTC relating to enforcement of subpoenas and temporary injunctions, and provided for expedition of court actions in antitrust cases.[6]

Pending Antitrust Enforcement Bills

Numerous antitrust proposals have been introduced during the present session of Congress. Senator Philip A. Hart (D-Mich.), chairman of the Senate Antitrust Subcommittee, observed recently that "a week does not pass without at least one colleague gracing the *Congressional Record* with admiring words for antitrust...."[7] In addition to the parens patriae bill (H.R. 8532), the following antitrust measures are receiving serious consideration in Congress:

- S. 1136, by Senators Hart, Hugh Scott (R-Pa.) and forty-odd cosponsors would authorize more than double the amounts available for antitrust enforcement activities over a period of three years. An amended version of this bill has been approved by the appropriate committees and the Senate is expected to act on the proposal during the current session of Congress. Another proposal (S. 449) by Senator John V. Tunney (D-Calif.) would authorize even higher appropriations.

- S. 1284 is an omnibus bill also cosponsored by Senators Hart and Scott. Hearings have been held on this bill, and committee action is expected during the current Congress. This proposal to "overhaul" the antitrust laws includes provisions to (1) broaden the Justice Department's powers to gather information relating to antitrust matters, (2) make a plea of "no contest" in a federal antitrust case admissible as prima facie evidence of a violation of antitrust law in a treble damage suit, (3) require large companies to notify the government before merging with other companies, and (4) authorize state attorneys general to bring civil antitrust damage suits on behalf of state citizens.

- S. 1959, the Hart Industrial Reorganization bill, is based on the author's view that "the antitrust laws were intended to eliminate monopolistic power just because it existed—because of the potential for abuse—because its mere existence was a restraint on competition."[8] This bill would make it unlawful "to possess monopoly power" and would create an industrial reorganization commission to prosecute violations before a special industrial reorganization court. The special court would be authorized to issue orders for the reorganization of corporations found to possess monopoly power if in its opinion this is necessary "to restore effective competition."[9] The bill also would establish a "presumption" that monopoly power is possessed if (1) there has been no substantial price competition among two or more corporations in any line of commerce for a period of three consecutive years out of the five most recent years, or (2) any four or fewer corporations account for 50 percent or more of sales in any line of commerce in any year out of the most recent three years. Thus the defendant would have the burden of rebutting such a presumption as provided in the bill. A divestiture of monopoly power would not be required, for example, if the defendant could show that it would result in loss of substantial economies.

- H.R. 6971 would nullify state "fair trade" laws which permit a manufacturer to specify a minimum resale price on a brand name product sold "in free and open competition" with similar products. Such minimum pricing agreements, sanctioned by Congress some three decades ago and reaffirmed with the approval of President Truman, are permitted under the antitrust laws wherever allowed by state law. H.R. 6971 passed the House on 21 July 1975 and a companion bill (S. 408) has been cleared by the Senate antitrust subcommittee and is awaiting action by the full Senate Committee on the Judiciary.

Purpose and Scope of the Antitrust Laws

The general objective of the antitrust laws, of course, is promotion of competition, or "fair rivalry," among businessmen. In order to promote this objective, the antitrust laws contain sweeping provisions directed against business "restraints" that may threaten a competitive economy. However, these statutes do not provide a precise description of prohibited activities. They are couched in broad terms and, for the most part, the terms are undefined.[10] A basic provision, for example, prohibits combinations "in restraint of trade," but Congress has left it to the courts to decide case by case what particular business practices fall under this rubric. Thus it has been said that the Sherman Antitrust Act states "a flexible public policy" and that even "a gargantuan catalog of possible antitrust sin would scarcely list all potential variations of irregular antitrust conduct."[11]

On the other hand, it should be noted that large segments of the economy are exempt, in varying degrees, from the antitrust laws. In other words, "Congress has decided that in some industries competition shall not be entirely free."[12] "While the right hand of our federal legislature has prohibited restraints of trade generally in our economy...its left hand, by special exemptions and regulatory statutes, has permitted such conduct in certain segments of industry and labor."[13] Thus the antitrust laws do not apply to certain anticompetitive conduct by various regulated industries (such as communication, transportation, and agriculture), by associations of exporters, and by labor unions.[14]

The basic principles embodied in the antitrust laws are contained in the Sherman Act of 1890[15] supplemented by the Clayton Act of 1914.[16] The parens patriae damage suits envisioned by H.R. 8532 could be based on a violation of any of the antitrust laws except section 2 (price discrimination) and section 7 (anticompetitive mergers) of the Clayton Act. However, the offense with which the parens patriae bill seems primarily concerned is price-fixing—an anticompetitive arrangement to increase or maintain the price of a product.[17] The committee report on the bill points out that the proposed suits may be based on overcharges attributable to various types of antitrust violations such as monopolization, boycotts, division of markets, exclusive dealings, tie-in arrangements, and conspiracies to limit production.[18]

SUMMARY OF THE BILL

The "Parens Patriae" Concept

The parens patriae bill would authorize any state attorney general to bring a damage suit in federal court on behalf of all persons residing in the state who may have been injured by an alleged violation of the federal antitrust laws.

Under the common law of England the term "parens patriae" (parent of the state) described the king's power as guardian. Thus, for example, a representative of the sovereign acted as parens patriae on behalf of certain individuals, such as incompetents and orphans, unable to represent themselves.[19] The parens patriae concept has been recognized and expanded in certain types of cases in our state courts, but federal antitrust laws do not authorize its use in treble damage suits on behalf of individuals.[20] Thus the Ninth Circuit Court of Appeals has ruled that the state of California could not maintain such an action.[21] However, the court observed that the state was "on the track of a suitable answer" and disclaimed any intent to discourage its search for a solution. Accordingly, the author of the bill argues that there is a need for "expanding the States' parens patriae powers under the antitrust laws."[22] A similar procedure under existing law permits private attorneys to bring a "class action" on behalf of one or more claimants and all others similarly situated.

The pending parens patriae bill (H.R. 8532) was introduced by Representative Peter W. Rodino, Jr. (D-N.J.), chairman of the House Committee on the Judiciary. Following subcommittee hearings on an earlier version of the proposal, the committee amended the bill and reported it to the House. A similar proposal is included in a Senate bill (S. 1284) introduced by Senators Hart and Scott.

Provisions of H.R. 8532

The pending bill, as reported to the House, may be summarized as follows:

Actions by State Attorneys General. Any state attorney general would be authorized to bring a civil action in federal court on behalf of any residents of his state who may have been damaged by an alleged violation of the federal antitrust laws. The bill would not permit a state attorney general to farm out such cases to private attorneys on a contingent fee basis.

Treble Damages. If a violation of the federal antitrust laws were established, the state, as parens patriae, would be entitled to recover "threefold the damages and the cost of suit, including a reasonable attorney's fee."

Notice by Publication. Notice to all persons in the state on whose behalf such a suit is filed would be given by publication in accordance with applicable state law, or in whatever manner the court specified.

Exclusion of Claimants upon Request. Any claimant could elect not to be represented by the attorney general and could be excluded from such a suit by filing a request within sixty days after notice of the suit is given. Any person in the class involved who failed to file such a notice (except for good cause) would be bound by the decision of the court.

No Compromises without Court Approval. Suits brought under the proposed statute could not be dismissed or compromised without approval of the court.

Estimation of Damages. The court would be permitted to determine the lump sum to be recovered by the state by any "reasonable system of estimating aggregate damages" without requiring separate proof by the individuals on whose behalf a suit is brought. Thus the bill provides that damages could be assessed "in the aggregate by statistical or sampling methods."

Distribution of Damages. The amounts recovered would be distributed by the state "in such manner as the district court may in its discretion authorize" provided that each person is given "a reasonable opportunity to secure his appropriate portion. . . ."

Assistance by the U.S. Attorney General. Whenever the attorney general of the United States files an antitrust suit and believes that any state attorney general would be entitled to bring a class action based substantially on the same alleged violation, he would notify the state attorney general. In addition, the U.S. attorney general would be required to make available to the state authorities any relevant investigative files and other materials to the extent permitted by law.

Proposals Not in the Bill

Damage to the General Economy. The bill does not include a provision, contained in an earlier version (H.R. 38), to permit recovery of damages for "injury to the general economy" of the state, or to any subdivision of the state, brought about by an antitrust violation.

Parens Patriae Suits by the U.S. Attorney General. An earlier version of the bill included a provision to authorize the attorney general of the United States to bring a parens patriae suit on behalf of the residents of a state if the state attorne general declines to do so. Such an action would be triggered if an antitrust suit for injury to the federal government were filed and a state attorney general declined to bring a parens patriae suit based substantially on the same alleged violation.

Defendant's Costs. The pending proposal, as reported, does not provide that if the defendant prevails—is absolved—he shall be entitled to reimbursement for the expenses incurred in defending himself. Thus if the defendant is absolved he must pay his costs including attorney fees, and if he does not prevail he must pay his costs plus the state's costs and fees in addition to treble damages.

Judicial Discretion. The House Judiciary Committee rejected an amendment to permit the courts to exercise discretion in awarding damages. The amendment would have permitted the courts to take into consideration the defendant's degree of culpability, any history of prior such conduct, ability to pay, effect on ability to continue to do business and such other matters as justice may require.[23]

THE MAIN ARGUMENTS

Compensation for Consumers

Supporting Arguments. The report on the bill, reflecting the views of a majority of the Judiciary Committee, summarizes the relationship between consumers and antitrust offenses in the following terms:

> The economic burden of many antitrust violations is borne in large measure by the consumer in the form of higher prices for his goods and services. This is especially true of such common and widespread practices as price-fixing, which usually result in higher prices for the consumer, regardless of the level in the chain of distribution at which the violation occurs. . . .Moreover, antitrust violations almost always contribute to inflation. They introduce illegal and artificial forces into the market place, thus undermining our economic system of free enterprise.
>
> Frequently, antitrust violations injure thousands or even millions of consumers, each in relatively small amounts. Indeed, many of the Justice Department's recent prosecutions have involved price-fixing of consumer goods on a local or regional basis.[24]

To illustrate the types of consumer items involved, the report refers to complaints alleging small overcharges on items such as snack foods, soft drinks, and bakery and dairy products. In such situations, because the small overcharges involved would not justify a damage suit by an individual purchaser, the present law permits a "class action" on behalf of all purchasers who claim to have been overcharged on a particular item. Such actions are authorized by rule 23 of the Federal Rules of Civil Procedure. One or more complainants may file a class action on behalf of all persons similarly situated. But advocates of the bill say that the present class action remedy is too restrictive when numerous small claimants are involved. Many courts have found that consumer class actions covering innumerable small individual claims present insurmountable problems of "manageability" in the conduct of the litigation. These manageability problems include proper notice, the complexity of evidentiary issues, and distribution of any recoveries. For example, under the present law notices must be provided to all identifiable persons on whose behalf the suit is brought. Where large numbers of potential claimants are involved, the cost of providing such notices may be prohibitive. The director of the Bureau of Competition in the Federal Trade Commission, James Halverton, has explained the impact of the notice requirement as construed by the Supreme Court in the case of *Eisen* v. *Carlisle and Jacquelin*:

The practical effect of *Eisen* is to eliminate the Rule 23 class action as a feasible means for recovery by a large class of individuals each of whom has sustained relatively minor damages. In situations where the costs of giving notice to the class are much greater than any individual class member's stake in the outcome of the action, it is unlikely that any suit will be brought. The person who deals in certain types of consumer goods, where each transaction may involve only a few dollars, can now fix prices, relatively free from the fear of substantial treble damage actions.

A description of the facts in *Eisen* will indicate where the Supreme Court's decision has left the consumer class action. The plaintiff, in *Eisen,* who claimed personal damages of only $70, sought to represent a class of as many as 6 million persons who allegedly were injured as a result of violations of the antitrust and securities laws. It was calculated that the cost of giving individual notice to all identifiable members of the class would be about $315,000. The Court, in ruling that the plaintiff must give such notice, explicitly recognized that its decision sounded the death knell for Eisen's class action because the plaintiff was unlikely to expend $315,000 to proceed with a suit in which he had a stake of only $70. The immediate result was that the defendants retained the profits from their allegedly illegal activities.[25]

The bill attempts to deal with the notice question by authorizing notice by "publication" if this is "the best notice practicable under the circumstances." Under the bill, attempts to notify potential claimants would be made by radio and television as well as by traditional newspaper advertisements.

Another group action problem dealt with in the bill relates to proof of total damages and of individual claims. The bill provides that total damages may be determined in the aggregate by statistical or sampling methods or by such other method as the court may deem reasonable. Thus total damages (overcharges) could be estimated on the basis of total sales instead of on proof of individual claims. This aggregation approach, it is argued, is necessary because "proof of individual claims and amounts would be impracticable and virtually impossible."[26]

On the question of how the damages recovered may be distributed among claimants, the bill leaves it to the courts to devise a distribution procedure that affords each person "a reasonable opportunity to secure his appropriate portion." Because many potential claimants are not expected to come forward to secure their shares, proponents of the bill anticipate that the amounts recovered will be substantially in excess of the amount distributed to claimants. Such amounts as may be left over would be used, in the courts' discretion, "for some public purposes benefiting, as closely as possible, the class of injured persons."[27] The committee report states that the proposed distribution procedure thus adopts a concept developed in highly imaginative fashion by a number of courts over the years. The judicial antecedents of section 4E include cases in which recoveries for illegal overcharges on bus and taxi fares were applied to reduce those fares in future years, and the innovative application of illegal overcharges in the antibiotic drug industry to a variety of programs beneficial to the drug-consuming public. These include the expansion of State-sponsored health programs, medical research, the training of nurses and paramedical personnel, the staffing of medical and rehabilitation clinics, and other similar programs.[28]

The bill does not indicate how the "appropriate portion" of each claimant is to be determined, and the report rejects "the notion...that each of millions of potential claimants for individually trivial sums be paraded through the court to prove his personal damages...."[29] The report explains that

parens patriae actions will normally be brought in instances where thousands or millions of consumers have been injured. Few consumers keep receipts for all the goods and services they purchase or use. In fact, individual receipts or records are not available on a great many consumer goods and services. Snack food machines, for instance, do not issue receipts.[30]

Thomas Kauper, assistant attorney general in charge of the antitrust division, testified on the proposed procedure for estimating and distributing damages as follows:

There is little doubt that scientific methods of measuring damages through statistical sampling and other devices are available. In addition, at least in the context of Sherman Act violations, we see little merit in the proposition that one whose antitrust liability is established is entitled to retain the proceeds of his illegal acts, absent a definitive showing by each individual damaged of both that fact and the precise amount of injury....

In an action where the State is representing its damaged citizens, the State would seem—as the bill provides—to be an appropriate receiver of the damages, subject to the rights of all damaged parties to claim their pro rata share. Finally, to the extent that any moneys recovered are not fully claimed by injured individuals, the use of the fund according to State law or pursuant to the doctrine of *cy pres* under the direction of the district court seems to me to be the most appropriate provision imaginable.[31]

Opposing Arguments. Seven of the minority members of the House Judiciary Committee oppose the proposal and their dissenting views are summarized in the House report.[32]

Among other things, the minority members are not convinced that the bill deals with a really substantial consumer problem. They point out that the typical case envisioned by advocates of the bill would involve only "trivial" compensation for each of the consumers involved. An illustration referred to in the report on the bill relates to an overcharge due to price-fixing of one dollar per item, and another example, cited by Assistant Attorney General Kauper, refers to cases involving overcharges on a consumer product "that may cost as little as 25 or 30 cents." In the absence of a mandatory statute separate damage suits to recover such trivial amounts would doubtless be dismissed under the doctrine of *de minimis non curat lex* (the law does not take notice of very small or trifling matters).

In response to the charge that unlawful price-fixing is "a common and widespread" practice, critics of the bill point out that the committee report does not document this assertion, and they argue that the statistics furnished by the Department of Justice during the committee hearings[33] do not support it. The head of the antitrust division testified that it has been his policy to generally seek criminal indictments for price-fixing wherever the evidence was sufficient.[34] Yet, although it is estimated that there are about 180,000 corporations in the United States (excluding those with annual sales under $1 million) with total sales in excess of $1 trillion, in fiscal 1974 the antitrust division was able to uncover only twenty-one cases in which evidence of price-fixing was sufficient to warrant prosecutions under the antitrust laws.

In twenty other cases there was "a real question as to the willfulness of a violation" and so these took the form of civil complaints. The government did not regard these as willful offenses because they involved pricing activities over a period of time with "the knowledge or approval of the regulatory authorities" and cases where "there is some reasonable question" as to whether the activities were within exemptions granted by law.[35] Moreover, it should be noted that the statistics furnished by the antitrust division cover "cases filed," and these, of course, do not show whether any of the alleged price-fixing violations stood up in court. A study of the eleven federal price-fixing cases in which a decision was reached in 1968 concluded that "only two resulted in litigated action," and one of these was dismissed because of insufficient evidence. The other nine cases were disposed of with the government's consent and without penalty by the issuance of cease and desist orders.[36]

The Department of Justice has indicated that "it would be almost impossible to predict with any real degree of accuracy" how many suits would be brought under the bill.[37] Assuming, however, that state attorneys general would be more successful than the U.S. attorney general in uncovering price-fixing violations under the federal antitrust laws, the dissenting members of the committee suggest that generally the amounts recovered "will not go to compensate victims," but "will be put to some noble purpose at the discretion of the court."[38] Although the bill provides that each potential claimant must be given a reasonable opportunity to secure his "appropriate portion" of the damages recovered, the proponents of the bill concede that rarely, if ever, will all potential claimants actually come forward to secure their share. Thus any amounts left over after satisfaction of individual claims would be distributed "for some public purpose" as the court may direct. The report states that the consumer who purchases a relatively inexpensive item—the purchaser with whom the bill is primarily concerned—"will almost certainly have no proof that he purchased the item at a particular time, place and price"[39] and that proof of such small claims would be "virtually impossible." Accordingly, the dissenters contend that generally there will be no provable known victims to compensate.

The dissenting members point out that in any event the bill does not provide for the filing and processing of damage suits by consumers. They assert that the bill relates to cases "where the claimants are often nameless, unidentified, unidentifiable, and ignorant of the trivial injury allegedly suffered and ignorant of who inflicted it."[40] Thus it is argued that the bill is not really a consumer proposal; that the "payments exacted from defendants...may be more accurately termed 'fines' than damage awards."[41]

Deterrence of Violations

Supporting Arguments. A basic purpose of the bill is to deter violations by preventing "unjust enrichment" of offenders. Accordingly, the question discussed here is whether the proposed treble damage penalties are necessary and appropriate measures for deterring violations of the antitrust laws.

The committee report on the bill assumes that additional deterrents are needed. Thus it does not discuss the deterrents available under the present antitrust laws. The report quotes Assistant Attorney General Kauper on the question of deterrence as follows:

> There can be no doubt that the treble damage remedy provides a strong deterrent, especially against price-fixing and other hard-core per se offenses. This damage remedy has been particularly effective in cases involving large purchasers. . . .
>
> I believe that there is a need for the availability of a method by which damages can be recovered where antitrust violations have caused small individual damages to large numbers of citizen-consumers. Without such a procedure, those antitrust violations which have the broadest scope and, often, the most direct impact on consumers would be most likely to escape the penalty of the loss of illegally-obtained profits....As a result, the goal of deterrence sought by the Clayton Act would be frustrated in those

situations where damages fell directly on small consumers or purchasers.[42]

Another antitrust enforcement official, the director of the Bureau of Competition of the Federal Trade Commission, has suggested, "The best deterrent to a resumption of the illegal [anticompetitive] conduct might be a suit by the state which deprives the violator of the profits gained from his bad conduct...."[43] The committee report also quotes from an opinion of the Ninth Circuit Court of Appeals which held that the state of California could not maintain a parens patriae action under the antitrust laws:

> The State most persuasively argues that it is essential that this sort of proceeding be made available if antitrust violations of the sort here alleged are to be rendered unprofitable and deterred. It would indeed appear that the State is on the track of a suitable answer (perhaps the most suitable yet proposed) to problems bearing on antitrust deterrence and the class action as a means of consumer protection. We disclaim any intent to discourage the State in its search for a solution.[44]

The majority members of the committee assert that a fundamental premise of the bill is that

> the antitrust laws should, at a minimum, provide an effective means whereby a plaintiff or plaintiff class can force a guilty defendant to part with all measurable fruits of his illegal activity as it relates to the plaintiff, multiplied threefold to reflect the factor Congress has determined is necessary as a punishment, as a deterrent, and as an incentive. This premise is in full accord with established concepts of damages under the antitrust laws. The cases reiterate that defendants must disgorge ill-gotten gains; and the standard rules for measuring damages allow a reasonable estimate thereof once the fact of injury has been established. . . .
>
> The committee believes that a defendant who has committed an antitrust violation has no right, constitutional or otherwise, to the retention of one penny of measurable illegal overcharges or other fruits of the violation. This committee emphatically rejects the notion that our constitutional requirements are so rigid that they somehow require that each of millions of potential claimants for individually trivial sums be paraded through the court to prove his personal damages, when the best evidence and often the only appropriate measure of the scope of the violation is found in the records of the defendants themselves. A number of Federal courts have agreed.[45]

Opposing Arguments. Although the majority report emphasizes the view that massive parens patriae actions for treble damages would deter antitrust violations, it does not discuss the other deterrents available under the present antitrust laws. Critics of the bill argue, in effect, that the treble damage penalty is no longer necessary or appropriate to deter antitrust offenses.

As indicated above, the antitrust authority Jerrold G. Van Cise has pointed out that the antitrust laws entail "multiple damnations" of forbidden conduct, "one punishment sure if another fails."[46] Although he feels that on balance the antitrust laws have been "salutary to our society," Van Cise has observed that individuals and corporations "are being subjected to increasingly severe punishment for debatable infractions of the antitrust laws." He describes the penalties that may be imposed as a result of a Justice Department proceeding in the following passage taken from *The Federal Antitrust Laws:*

> In such a proceeding, fines may be imposed on each corporate and individual defendant for each violation of a section of the Sherman Act. Such fines are not tax deductible and possibly may not be reimbursable by the corporate employer. Additional consequences for individual defendants may include surrender to the custody of the U.S. marshall, fingerprinting, posting of bonds, sentencing, handcuffs, and a term in jail. The cumulative nature of these criminal penalties in the past is illustrated by the *Safeway* proceeding in which a corporate defendant was fined a total of $105,000 and a principal executive was both fined $75,000 and placed on probation with two concurrent one-year jail sentences. Similarly, in the electrical companies case, the corporate defendants were fined a total of $1,787,000, their executives were fined an aggregate of $137,500, and seven of these executives received and served 30-day jail sentences. In the future, by reason of a 1974 amendment of the Sherman Act, violation of this statute may result in a fine not to exceed $1 million if the defendant is a corporation, a fine not to exceed $100 thousand if the defendant is an individual person, and imprisonment for a term not to exceed three years in the case of such an individual person—plus attendant loss of civil rights.
>
> As remarked by Judge Knox in the *Carboloy* case:
>
> "Undoubtedly the temper of the country has changed and the temper of the judiciary has changed over what it was twenty or twenty-five years ago, and I suppose that industry must adjust itself to such changes and those who are in executive positions in large businesses must realize the need to conform to present day mores. One of them I suppose is that in interstate commerce in a large industry, price-fixing is taboo, and those who engage in it run serious risk of being severely punished."[47]

The Department of Justice may also bring a civil action that parallels a criminal action directed to the same violation, and it may be pursued even though the criminal action is decided adversely to the government. The deterrent potential of civil actions also is described by Van Cise:

> At the conclusion of such a civil action a defendant may find himself required to deal where he does not want to deal, license where he does not wish to license, surrender contractual and other rights, and be subjected in perpetuity to government visitations. The court injunction, moreover, may order the divestiture of stock or of assets, and even the outright dissolution of offending organizations. Further relief may subsequently be ordered.
>
> In short, the department is not limited to requesting, in a civil proceeding, the mere cessation of past objectionable conduct: "When the purpose to restrain trade appears from a clear violation of law, it is not necessary that all of the untraveled roads to that end be left open and that only the worn one be closed."[48]

Many years ago, when the maximum fine under the antitrust laws was only $5,000, it was argued that the treble damage provision should be retained to supplement such a light penalty.[49] However, as indicated above, Congress has now increased the antitrust penalties tremendously. Hence it may be argued that mandatory treble damages are no longer justifiable on the ground that other penalties are inadequate.

Opponents of the bill have pointed out also that, in addition to the deterrents available under the present federal law, almost all of the states have their own antitrust laws. They ask why the states do not amend these laws if necessary to authorize parens patriae antitrust suits in their own courts. The attorney general of Alabama answered this question very candidly. He testified during the 1974 hearings that "attempts to persuade the state legislature to pass more comprehensive and effective antitrust legislation have been unsuccessful."[50] Hence critics of the bill ask the question, If the legislature of a state, acting for its citizens, is not convinced that the parens patriae concept is sound policy, should Congress bypass the legislature and provide the state attorney general with such a policy and access to the federal courts to enforce it? The answer, in the opinion of some commentators, is that "there is something fundamentally unsound in turning over the enforcement of the Federal antitrust laws to a State Attorney General."[51] Consistent with this view, some critics of the bill suggest that Congress authorize the Department of Justice to handle parens patriae cases, and they ask whether that isn't the most efficient manner of enforcing the federal antitrust laws.

Others have suggested that parens patriae antitrust cases be allocated according to the impact of the alleged violation, that the federal government focus on parens patriae damage cases with substantial interstate impact, and that a state be authorized to file suits on behalf of its residents in the event the federal government declines to do so.

The legal capacity of the states to enforce their own antitrust laws on behalf of their citizens has been described as follows:

> The States can address all antitrust problems which occur within the States, and there is no inhibition on their doing so even though it overlaps to some extent with Federal antitrust statutes. Certainly New York and other States have been bringing such antitrust actions, and almost all of the States are empowered to do so under very broad statutes. That is an important and developing area of antitrust enforcement, which I hope the States will concentrate on and not be detracted from....
>
> They do have criminal penalties. They have civil forfeitures and civil penalties. Some of the penalties are much greater than even under the Federal statutes. There have been State penalties imposed in some cases of over $1 million, and they have other Draconian remedies, such as forfeiting the right to do business, forfeiting your charter, forfeiting your right to public bidding, and the like, which give the States a very powerful arsenal. Of course, there is no reason why they can't enlarge their own remedies if they think it is necessary.[52]

Mandatory Treble Damages

Supporting Arguments. Advocates of the bill point out that an award of treble damages in a private antitrust suit is not a novel remedy; that the Sherman Act, adopted some eighty-five years ago, permits "any person" injured by an antitrust offense to prosecute such an action. Consumers who would be involved in a parens patriae suit already have the right to join in bringing suit for treble damages "even if, for practical reasons, the right to sue is not likely to be exercised."[53] Thus, proponents argue, the bill would simply provide a practical method "for the vindication of existing substantive claims."[54] Also, imposition of treble damages as proposed would provide an added deterrent because "the likelihood of a financial recovery against an antitrust violator...is significantly increased...."

The majority report states that those who violate the antitrust laws should be required to do more than return their "ill-gotten gains"—that actual damages should be "multiplied threefold to reflect the factor Congress had determined is necessary as a punishment, as a deterrent, and as an incentive. This premise is in full accord with established concepts of damages under the antitrust laws."[55] Consistent with this view, it has been argued that the other antitrust deterrents have not always been sufficient and that "there should be no weakening of the triple damage threat though it may, in individual cases, work injustice."[56]

Opposing Arguments. Opponents ask whether treble damages should be mandatory or be left to the trial judge's discretion, since an antitrust defendant may be faced with multiple penalties under the federal antitrust laws.

The dissenting members of the House Judiciary Committee assert that "[w]hat the treble damage award really is in this context is punishment. . . .But the fines imposed by this bill—and this is critical—may not be imposed commensurate with the interests of justice."[57] The dissenters go on to point out that

> the committee rejected an amendment that would have permitted the court to take into consideration the "defendant's degree of culpability, any history of prior such conduct, ability to pay, effect on ability to continue to do business and such other matters as justice may require." Although these actions may be filed on behalf of millions of unknown individuals and involve millions of dollars, the resultant award must be arbitrarily calculated and may not be reduced even if the interests of justice so require.[58]

The treble damage award was among the subjects explored in a comprehensive study of the antitrust laws by a committee selected in consultation with the attorney general at that time, Herbert Brownell, and President Eisenhower. The results of the study, which was conducted over a period of approximately two years, were published by the Department of Justice in 1955.[59]

The report of the attorney general's committee recommended a proposal "to substitute the trial judge's discretion to double or triple damage awards for the present mandatory treble damage requirement."[60] Among the points made in support of this view was that "the increased reach of antitrust sometimes traps unwitting violators" and that "to treat such unknowing transgressors on a par with willful wrongdoers seems arbitrary and unfair."[61]

The report of the attorney general's committee included the following criticisms of the mandatory treble damage approach:

> Many urge that making triple recovery discretionary will not impair the deterrent effect of private suits. For the conscious malefactor cannot expect the benefit of such discretion. And the unwitting violator, seeking to act in conformity with the law, is naturally unaffected by the threat of triple damages.
>
> Nor will incentive to private suit be curtailed. The inducement of mandatory trebled damages is no longer necessary to encourage suits by injured persons. The development of both the procedural and substantive law, largely favorable to the plaintiff, plus the award of attorney fees, affords sufficient incentive to private antitrust actions.

> Also, liberal requirements for proof of damages suggest that, even in the absence of mandatory trebling, plaintiffs may secure ample recompense. Thus the Supreme Court has held that, "though damages could not be measured with...exactness", a jury finding will be sustained. And, generally, once plaintiff shows any injury, juries may infer lost profits from plaintiff's past earnings or from current yields of similar enterprises. Finally, monopoly increases in plaintiff's costs may be inferred from estimates of what market price might have been under competitive conditions....
>
> On balance, we favor vesting in the trial judge discretion to impose double or treble damages. In all instances, this would recompense injured parties. Beyond compensation, the trial court could then penalize the purposeful violator without imposing the harsh penalty of multiple damages on innocent actors.[62]

The report points out that there is ample precedent for this approach; that other treble damage statutes provide for vesting discretionary power in the trial judge to award up to three times actual damages.[63] An appropriate penalty, the report stated, should be determined in the light of the circumstances.

> Discretion should turn on a variety of factors, including, for example, industry background, the business rationale for the challenged practices, the extent of injury, the legal advice preceding the challenged conduct and the record, if any, of past violations. These diverse factors are ill-suited to the statutory framework desirable for formulating any jury charge. They can best be considered by a court in the exercise of its sound judgment.
>
> We finally emphasize that this proposal in no way saps the enforcement strength of private suits. Such proceedings have a vital role to play in aiding understaffed Government agencies to enforce antitrust prohibitions throughout the Nation.[64]

A basic reason for the treble damage provision in the antitrust laws was to offer "private persons" an incentive to bring antitrust suits and thus to deter violations. As explained by the Senate Committee on the Judiciary some two decades ago, "the damages of 'persons' are trebled so that *private persons* will be encouraged to bring actions which, though brought to enforce a private claim, will nonetheless serve the public interest in the enforcement of the antitrust laws."[65] The committee then noted that a monetary incentive would be "wholly improper" in cases brought by government enforcement authorities. Accordingly, the committee explained that the antitrust laws "give the government the right to recover only actual, as distinguished from treble, damages."[66]

> This difference in treatment is a recognition of the difference in the position of the United States and of "persons" in this connection. . . . The damages of "persons" are trebled so that private persons will be encouraged to bring actions which, though brought to enforce a private claim, will nonetheless serve the public interest in the enforcement of the antitrust laws. The United States is, of course, charged by law with the enforcement of the antitrust laws and it would be wholly improper to write into the statute a provision whose chief purpose is to promote the institution of proceedings. The United States is, of course, amply equipped with the criminal and civil process with which to enforce the antitrust laws.[67]

Consistent with this reasoning, it may be argued that one of the basic justifications for awarding treble damages—the encouragement of private parties to help enforce the antitrust laws—would not be applicable to antitrust suits brought by a state government under the parens patriae bill.

The real incentive for state attorneys general to bring antitrust damage suits under the bill, opponents say, is a "political incentive."

> [W]e believe that the bill will be subject to much abuse. By calling on the State attorneys to champion these antitrust actions, the bill seeks to provide a political incentive for antitrust enforcement in cases where even treble damage awards provide no economic incentive.
>
> We believe that politics and antitrust will not make a happy marriage. The temptations for the politically ambitious to ride into the public eye as its champion against "fat cat" antitrust violators by filing lawsuits to the sound of political trumpets may be too great. Since antitrust cases take years to complete, the politically ambitious attorney general need not fear the embarrassment of a string of losses. In any event, many of the cases will have been undoubtedly settled because of their adverse publicity and their nuisance value. This bill underscores how quickly we have forgotten the lesson many thought we learned last year that politics and antitrust should not be mixed.[68]

Costs and Attorney Fees: The Question of Fairness

As noted above, the parens patriae bill provides that if the court rules against a defendant he must pay the state, in addition to treble damages, its cost of the suit including attorneys' fees. On the other hand, if the court rules *for* the defendant, the bill does not permit him to recover his costs and fees even if he is the innocent victim of an untenable damage suit. Moreover, the bill [section 3(3)] would extend the right to attorneys' fees to prevailing plaintiffs—but not to prevailing defendants—in injunction cases as well as in treble damage suits.

Supporting Arguments. The House Judiciary Committee report on the bill states that the attorneys' fee provision "preserves the incentive for a private party to file a meritorious lawsuit." In other words, it is suggested that the bill would apply the incentive concept now applicable in private antitrust cases to parens patriae suits brought by state attorneys general. The rationale given for the attorneys' fee provision in the present antitrust laws, which is essentially the same as that given for the treble damage provision, is explained in the House committee report as follows:

> Because antitrust cases are frequently lengthy and complicated, they are normally very expensive for a person to bring and maintain. Attorneys' fees, therefore, comprise by far the largest portion of the legal expenses incurred in maintaining a private antitrust lawsuit. Since the award of attorneys' fees is made in addition to the treble damage award, a prevailing plaintiff is able to pay for the services of his attorney without having to reduce his damage award. The attorneys' fee provision thus preserves the incentive for a private party to file a meritorious lawsuit.[69]

Opposing Arguments. On the other hand, it may be argued that the allowance of attorneys' fees to a prevailing plaintiff (the state) while denying the court the power to award such costs to a prevailing defendant is manifestly unfair, and that Congress has recognized this in the enactment of various more modern statutes. Also, critics of the bill may point out that it would not provide an attorneys' fee incentive for "private parties" to bring damage suits. The parens patriae suits would be brought by state attorneys general "whose duty is to promote the public interest."[70] It may be noted in this connection that the attorneys' fee provision in the existing law does not apply in antitrust damage cases brought by the U.S. attorney general. Some two decades ago the House Judiciary Committee pointed out that "unlike the situation with respect to private persons, there is no need to furnish the Government any special incentive to enforce the antitrust laws, a heavy responsibility with which it is already charged."[71]

The Supreme Court, in a case decided 12 May 1975, declined on its own motion to adopt a general rule for awarding attorneys' fees "based on the private attorney general approach when such judicial rule will operate *only against private parties and not against the Government.*"[72] And the Court noted that in some instances Congress has provided that attorneys' fees could be awarded to either party "depending upon the outcome of the litigation and the court's discretion."[73] The examples cited include the Civil Rights Act of 1964 and the rule applicable in treble damage suits under the patent laws. Both of these statutes bar attorneys' fee allowances for the government but give the courts discretion to award such fees to prevailing defendants. In fact, both statutes make it clear that the government "shall be liable for such fees the same as a private citizen."[74] Another and more recent departure from the fee award concept in the bill is contained in the Legal Services Corporation Act of 25 July 1974. In this act, Congress permitted the award of costs and attorneys' fees to a defendant when suits are filed maliciously or for the purpose of harassing the defendant.[75] Such costs and fees, the statute provides, shall be directly paid by the corporation.

Accordingly, it may be argued that the proposed attorneys' fee provision would be unfair to defendants and inappropriate for suits brought by state attorneys general. Congress seems to have recognized the unfairness of such a provision by authorizing damage suits under certain other legislation.

Cases Farmed Out by the States—Contingent Fees

The bill would not permit private attorneys to handle parens patriae cases for a state on a contingent fee basis. In other words, the fees paid such lawyers by a state could not be contingent upon whether the suit is successful, or based upon a percentage of the amount recovered.

Supporting Arguments. The committee report on the bill explained the rationale for this restriction as follows:

> The committee strongly supports the development of "inhouse" State antitrust capabilities. At the present time, regrettably, only a few States have the staff and financial ability to prosecute protracted antitrust cases without the assistance of retained private attorneys. Especially in consolidated multistate litigation, retained counsel may well be both necessary and entirely proper for parens patriae cases.
>
> Nonetheless, the Judiciary Committee believes that certain types of fee arrangements between States and private attorneys may inhibit the development of State antitrust capabilities. The definition of State attorney general, therefore, specifically prohibits parens patriae cases to be brought by "any person employed or retained on a contingency fee basis."
>
> Suits in the name of a State are an exercise of State power. The committee believes that the States should exercise control over the use of State power not only in theory but in fact. If a State attorney general were able to delegate this function to private counsel on a contingency fee basis, the political and financial stake he would experience in otherwise prosecuting the action would be substantially diminished. And thus State power would

be exercised without the guarantee of State supervision.

> The committee bill excludes the use of fee arrangements whereby a State agrees to pay a private attorney a percentage of the recovery if the attorney wins the parens patriae case for the State. H.R. 8532 also prohibits any contracts which make the outside counsel's fee or the amount thereof contingent on the amount, if any, of the recovery or on whether there is a recovery.[76]

Opposing Arguments. Representative Barbara Jordan (D-Texas), a member of the Judiciary Subcommittee on Monopolies and Commercial Law, argues that the contingent fee restriction "may have the effect of undermining a great deal of what the bill is intended to accomplish." Ms. Jordan, a strong supporter of the purpose of the bill, is "concerned that a flat ban on contingency fees will effectively place the services of perfectly ethical and highly knowledgeable attorneys beyond the reach of the States." It is unrealistic, in her view, to expect that more than a handful of states will have the resources to conduct a significant amount of antitrust litigation. Thus she argues that for the foreseeable future there will be a critical need for the services of the private bar if the bill is to have any real impact. Ms. Jordan suggests that contingent fees could be allowed subject to approval by the courts on a case by case basis and that there is nothing wrong with such an arrangement. Moreover, she favors federal aid to help the states develop antitrust capabilities.

Ms. Jordan also takes the position that the contingent fee is recognized as an important tool for weeding out frivolous and unmeritorious cases.

> Most plaintiff's antitrust litigation, like much plaintiff's litigation in general, is conducted presently on a contingent fee basis. Section 4 of the Clayton Act anticipates this. It provides for the court to award a reasonable attorney's fee to a prevailing plaintiff, in addition to his treble damage recovery. Thus for the most part, lawyers agree to take antitrust cases for plaintiffs in return for whatever fee the court awards them at the successful conclusion or settlement of the action. Without such arrangements, there would be precious little private antitrust enforcement, since few, if any, plaintiffs will be able to pay the normal hourly rate of experienced counsel without regard to the outcome of the case. States, while in a better financial position than ordinary private plaintiffs, will likewise be unable in most instances to commit the required sums to a major case in advance, win or lose.[77]

A proper contingent fee provision, Ms. Jordan concludes, would respond to two points made by critics of the bill. By weeding out questionable suits such a provision would (1) tend to prevent "a plethora of unfounded lawsuits," and (2) deter "politically ambitious state officials bent on making a reputation without regard to the ultimate disposition of the cases they bring."[78]

The contingent fee restriction is criticized also on the ground that it is dangerously ambiguous.

> It does not specify what contingent elements must be present in order to render an arrangement unacceptable, and it is clear that not all uncertainty as to final amount will render a fee "contingent." Even where the lawyer is being paid an hourly charge, he will usually have little idea at the outset what his actual fee will be. The committee amendment could, therefore, be open to an interpretation which would salvage fee contracts dependent for their ultimate amount on some unknown element, such as the award of the court at the conclusion of the case. The risk is very great, however, that a court would determine that the arrangement was "contingent" if some element of success—either at settlement or at trial—made the difference between a large fee for the lawyer and a low, probably uncompensatory one.[79]

NOTES TO TEXT

[1] U.S. Department of Justice, *Report of the Attorney General's National Committee to Study the Antitrust Laws,* 31 March 1955, p. 1.

[2] Jerrold G. Van Cise, *The Federal Antitrust Laws,* 3d ed. rev. (Washington, D.C.: American Enterprise Institute, 1975), p. 42.

[3] Ibid., p. 2.

[4] Ibid., p. 61.

[5] Public Law 93-528, approved 21 December 1974.

[6] Ibid.

[7] "Pressure Building for New Antitrust Laws," *Congressional Quarterly,* 12 July 1975, p. 1487.

[8] U.S. Congress, Senate, *Congressional Record,* vol. 121, 94th Cong., 1st sess. (17 June 1975), p. S 10731.

[9] Ibid., p. S 10735.

[10] Van Cise, *Federal Antitrust Laws,* p. 2.

[11] Ibid., p. 6.

[12] *Report of the Attorney General's National Committee,* p. 261.

[13] Van Cise, *Federal Antitrust Laws,* pp. 2-3.

[14] Ibid., p. 3; and *Report of the Attorney General's National Committee,* pp. 293-306. Other examples of antitrust immunities could be cited. For example, the Concessions Policy Act removes all competition from national park contracts. Thus, according to one observer, the government has agreed to the operation of vast recreational facilities by "companies who run them as legal monopolies, and increasingly these companies are big conglomerates." Arthur John Keefe with Ruth Wallick, "Legal Monopolies in the National Parks," *American Bar Association Journal,* vol. 61 (August 1975), pp. 979-980.

[15] Title 15 U.S. Code, sections 1-3.

[16] Title 15 U.S. Code, sections 13, 14, 18.

[17] U.S. Congress, House, Committee on the Judiciary, *Antitrust Parens Patriae Act,* Report No. 94-499 (cited hereafter as *House Report*), p. 3. See also testimony of Assistant Attorney General Thomas E. Kauper, Hearings before the Committee on the Judiciary, *Antitrust Parens Patriae Amendments,* 18 March 1974 (cited hereafter as *House Hearings*), p. 38.

[18] *House Report*, p. 3. For a description of the types of practices prohibited by the major provisions of the antitrust laws, see the 1975 edition of Van Cise's book, *The Federal Antitrust Laws*.

[19] *House Report*, p. 5.

[20] Ibid., pp. 4-6.

[21] Ibid., p. 8.

[22] *House Hearings*, p. 14.

[23] *House Report*, p. 24.

[24] Ibid., pp. 3-4.

[25] Ibid., p. 7.

[26] Ibid., p. 14.

[27] Ibid., p. 16.

[28] Ibid.

[29] Ibid., p. 15.

[30] Ibid., p. 4.

[31] *House Hearings*, pp. 20-21.

[32] *House Report*, pp. 23-25.

[33] *House Hearings*, p. 44.

[34] Ibid.

[35] Ibid.

[36] James W. Meehan, Jr. and H. Michael Mann, "Antitrust Policy and Allocative Efficiency: Incompatible?" (Paper presented at a seminar on Problems of Regulation and Public Utilities, Dartmouth College, 30 August 1973), pp. 37-38.

[37] *House Hearings*, p. 36.

[38] *House Report*, p. 23.

[39] Ibid., p. 6.

[40] Ibid., p. 23.

[41] Ibid.

[42] *House Hearings*, p. 19.

[43] *House Report,* p. 5.

[44] Ibid., p. 8.

[45] Ibid., pp. 13-14.

[46] Van Cise, *Federal Antitrust Laws,* p. 42.

[47] Ibid., pp. 43-44.

[48] Ibid., p. 45.

[49] *Report of the Attorney General's National Committee,* p. 379.

[50] *House Hearings,* p. 62.

[51] U.S. Congress, House, Committee on the Judiciary, *Antitrust Parens Patriae Amendment,* Hearings before the Subcommittee on Monopolies and Commercial Law, 94th Congress, 1st sess. (6 March 1975), p. 82.

[52] Ibid., p. 62.

[53] *House Report,* p. 9.

[54] Ibid.

[55] Ibid., p. 14.

[56] *Report of the Attorney General's National Committee,* p. 379.

[57] *House Report,* p. 23.

[58] Ibid., p. 24.

[59] *Report of the Attorney General's National Committee,* p. iv.

[60] Ibid., pp. 378-79.

[61] Ibid., p. 378.

[62] Ibid., pp. 378-79.

[63] Ibid., p. 380.

[64] Ibid.

[65] U.S. Congress, Senate, Committee on the Judiciary, Report No. 619, 84th Cong., 1st sess. (21 June 1955), p. 3., italics added.

[66] Ibid.

[67] Ibid.

[68] *House Report,* pp. 24-25.

[69] Ibid., p. 19.

[70] Ibid., p. 5.

[71] U.S. Congress, House, Committee on the Judiciary, Report No. 422, 18 April 1955.

[72] Alyeska Pipeline Service Company v. The Wilderness Society, 44 L Ed 2d, 141, 144 (1975). Italics added. The Court noted that "an award against a state government would raise a question with respect to its permissibility under the Eleventh Amendment, a question on which the lower courts are divided."

[73] Ibid., p. 141, note 37.

[74] See Title 42, United States Code, sections 2000a-3(b), 2000e-5(k) and Title 35, United States Code, section 285.

[75] See Title 42, United States Code, section 2996e(f).

[76] *House Report,* p. 18.

[77] Ibid., p. 27.

[78] Ibid., p. 28.

[79] Ibid.